Y0-CVL-699

A Gift For:

....

From:

....

Copyright © 2011 Hallmark Licensing, Inc.

Published by Hallmark Gift Books,
a division of Hallmark Cards, Inc.,
Kansas City, MO 64141
Visit us on the Web at www.Hallmark.com.

All rights reserved. No part of this publication
may be reproduced, transmitted, or stored in any
form or by any means without the prior written
permission of the publisher.

Writer: Dan Taylor
Editor: Chelsea Fogleman
Art Director: Kevin Swanson
Designer: Bryan Ring
Production Artist: Dan Horton

ISBN: 978-1-59530-341-7
BOK3119

Printed and bound in China

THE GIFT OF
Getting COOL STUFF

Hallmark
GIFT BOOKS

THE GIFT OF
Getting COOL STUFF

You deserve to get yourself the perfect thing. The kind of thing that's so perfect that only you could have picked it out.

But you don't want to go to a bunch of stores and waste time looking at all kinds of things. That's just too many things.

So that's why you're getting this handy guide that will help you narrow down, prioritize, and laser focus on what you want to get (which might even be a laser focuser!).

There's a popular idea that guys don't like shopping. This is not true. Before they were anything, guys were hunters and gatherers. And they still enjoy hunting for bargains and gathering "guest reward" points that will add up to a free dessert or possibly a nylon jacket.

So as you get ready to pick out something really cool for yourself, let's look at a few of the most popular places a guy can shop...

NOTE: Places men do not shop include the Candle Store, Fabric Store, and some kind of combination Candle and Fabric Store.

PLACE WITH COOL STUFF
HARDWARE STORE

....

This is the Holy Grail of shopping for guys. In fact,
it's where you would find the stuff to make your own grail.
It literally does not matter if a guy knows what he's looking
at—if it's in a Hardware Store, it's interesting.

It's especially interesting if it's new and improved.
Or bigger. Or "now with more power."

And there are a few key areas of the Hardware Store
that are worth paying extra attention to...

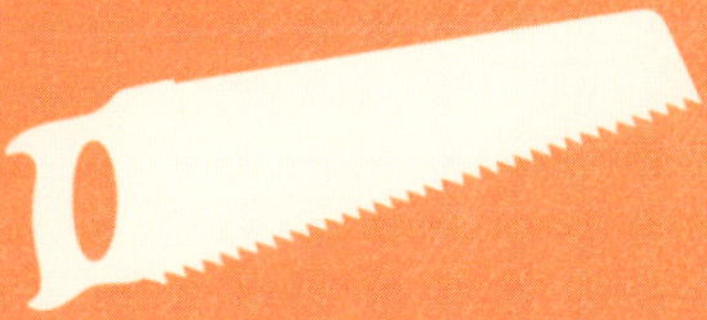

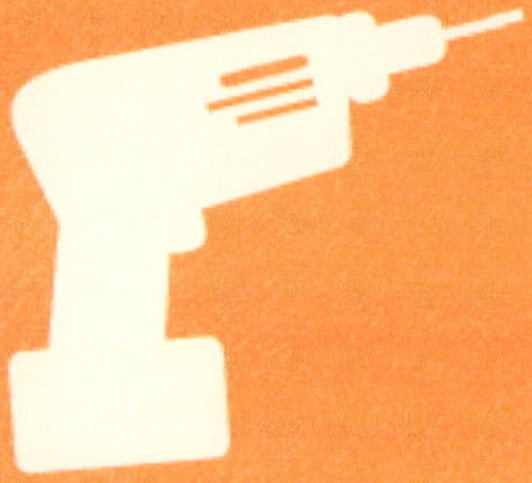

PLACE WITH COOL STUFF
HARDWARE STORE

· ·

TOOL AISLE

Insulated grip pliers? Metric ratchet sets are a must,
but do you also have whatever isn't metric?
Can you gap your spark plugs?
Not without the right hand tools you can't!

Allen wrenches! Where are your Allen wrenches?!
Not to mention adjustable wrenches, pipe wrenches,
open-end wrenches, box-end wrenches,
and underwater laser wrenches...

PLACE WITH COOL STUFF
HARDWARE STORE

LAWN CARE SECTION: SUMMER

We are at war.

TARGET: WEEDS

Propelling yourself across the battlefield, it's difficult not to swell with pride and a sense of accomplishment. The only thing better is to ride across said battlefield in a zero-turn radius tank with a 42-inch cutting deck, headlights, and a cup holder. Hand-to-hand skirmishes call for a good weed whacker and maybe a couple gallons of weed killer to wipe out stragglers.

LAWN CARE SECTION: WINTER

We are at war.

TARGET: SNOW AND ICE

Blowing that snow 45 feet from where it wants to be
is the single greatest accomplishment of mankind—
and it can be accomplished by you! Hand-to-hand skirmishes
call for shovels and possibly a butane torch (which is
in another section of the store but is still awesome).

PLACE WITH COOL STUFF
ELECTRONICS STORE

Scientists are now working to make a flatter screen than the flattest flat screen you've ever seen. There is a computer monitor that makes you feel like you're standing behind the computer! And have you heard about the mouse that's an actual mouse? It's amazing! Let's not even get started on the latest video games, or we'll be here all day.

The point is—you need electronics, and you know where to find them.

"Early Adopters" are people in the know before anyone else even knows there's anything to know. If you are such a person, you are probably reading this through the lenses of your cold fusion-generating, antigravity-supporting, X-ray-vision electronic glasses or something.

And if you're not an Early Adopter yet, you can become one by hitting the Electronics Store right now! Use the GPS on your watch to find it and go!

PLACE WITH COOL STUFF
GOLF OR PRO SHOP

....

What separates you from professional golfers? Clearly, it's equipment.

Your natural ability has been evident since 4th grade. You've got the patience, the steely nerves, and the killer instincts. Now all you need is the right club! Or clubs. Or bag. Or shoes. Or range finder. Or hat. Or balls. Or tees. Or stand bag, cart bag, or travel bag. Possibly a cart. With a cooler and satellite readouts providing continuous coverage of that cloud bank over the clubhouse...

All of this, plus tips, plus much, much more is waiting for you at the Golf or Pro Shop.

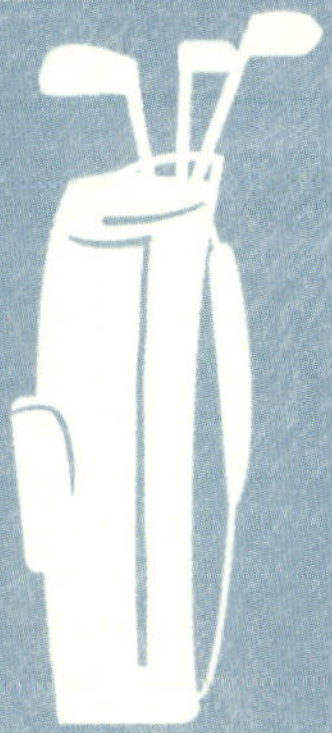

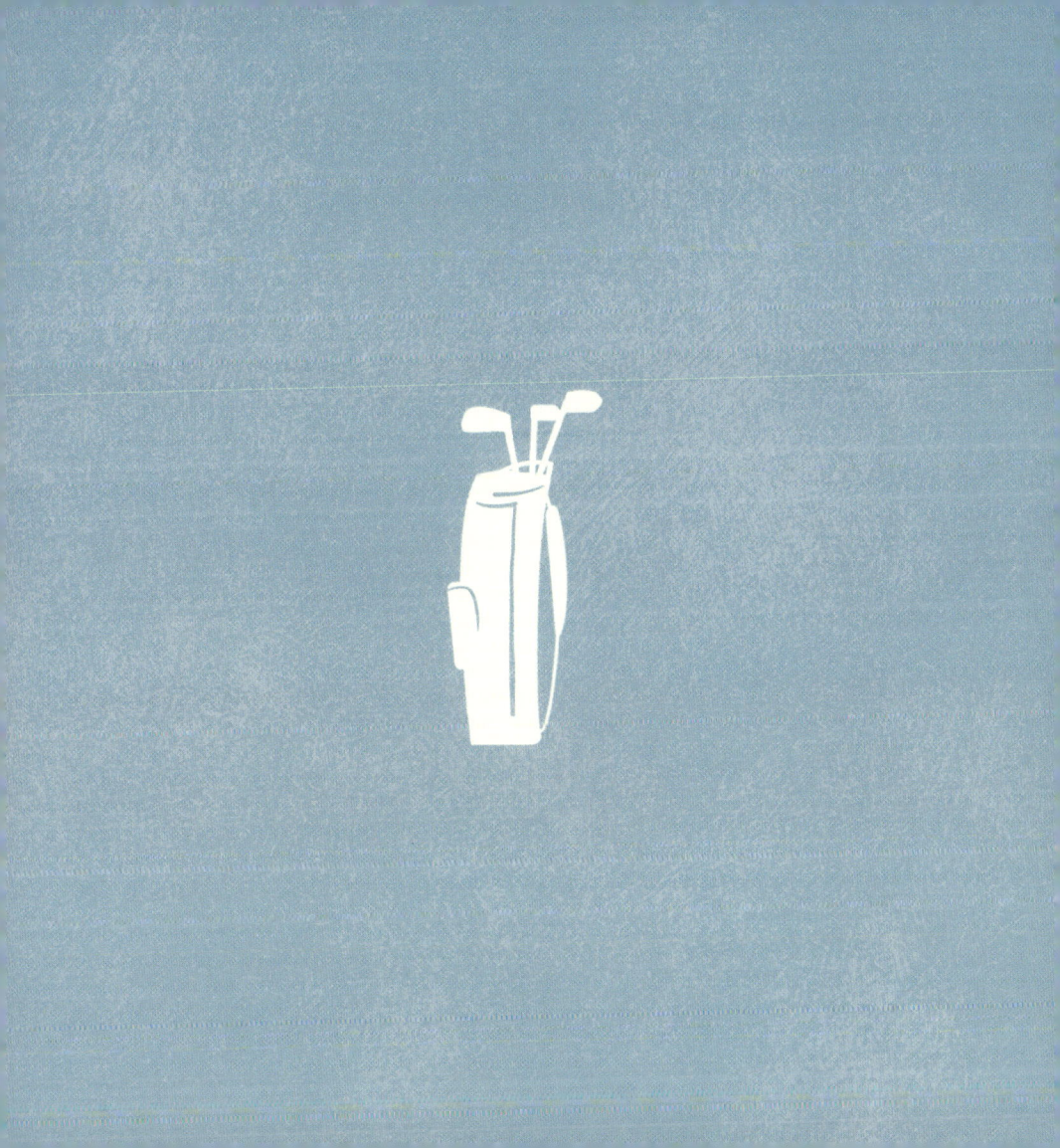

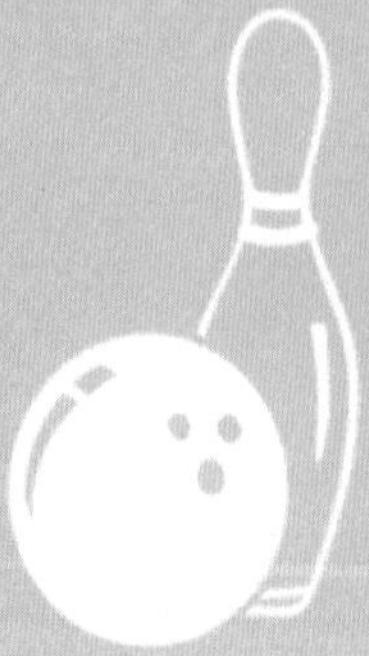

PLACE WITH COOL STUFF
SPORTING GOODS STORE

....

Like the hallowed Hardware Store, the Sporting Goods Store is divided into separate sections of shopping splendor.

There are sections for you to get stuff to:

- **KILL MOSQUITOES IN A LARGER CIRCUMFERENCE.**
- **MAKE YOU EVEN MORE INVISIBLE IN THE WOODS.**
- **PROCLAIM YOUR TEAM LOYALTY IN A WAY THAT CAN BE SEEN FROM SPACE.**

Yes, the Sporting Goods Store has so many amazing departments, it's hard to know where to start.

But we'll try.

PLACE WITH COOL STUFF
SPORTING GOODS STORE

....

FISHING SECTION

For a true fisherman, nothing calms you down, focuses your busy mind, and just makes you glad to be alive like sitting very still and waiting for a long time.

But doubt can cloud the clear mental sky that keeps you at your best. Your focus can be undermined with questions like: Are my jigs and gigs and rigs up to date? Is my spinner spinning? Is my finder finding anything? Is my hat ridiculous enough?

If the answer to any of those questions is "no," then you need to head to the fishing section to see what's biting.

And speaking of getting bitten…

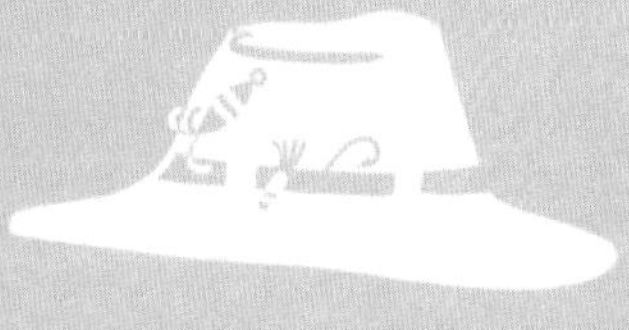

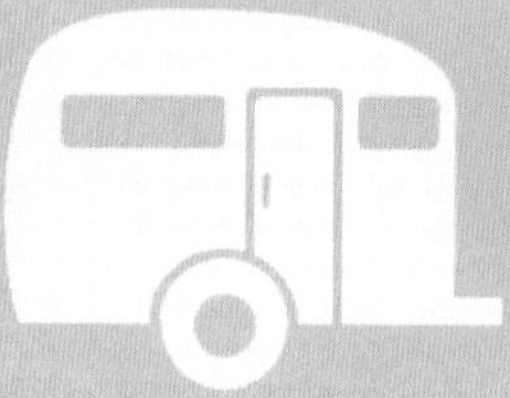

PLACE WITH COOL STUFF
SPORTING GOODS STORE

....

CAMPING SECTION

The goal of camping, as every camper knows, is to be as much outdoors in nature as you can—without being too much outdoors in nature. That's why the camping section of the sporting goods store is stocked with coolers, grills, lanterns, generators, and gallons upon gallons of bug spray.

You can shop to your heart's content, but remember that real guys don't ever refer to those tiny demonstrator tents as "adorable." (They are, of course, but guys don't say that.)

PLACE WITH COOL STUFF
SPORTING GOODS STORE

TEAM LOGO SECTION

"What to wear?" is a question that guys don't usually ponder.

Except when it comes to that one very deep,
all-important clothing question...
"What team logo should be on what I wear?"

Do you want to represent a local community team
or the team from your larger region? Do you want
to represent your college? Or do you want to go rogue
and wear the gear of an enemy, a villain, a hated rival?
Regardless of what you choose, options are available in
a wide array of colors, styles, and price ranges!

If guys were ever going to shop for clothes,
this would be where they'd start.

GO, TEAM!

PLACE WITH COOL STUFF
ANYWHERE FOOD IS SERVED

Of course, guys don't like grocery shopping.
But ordering food at restaurants? Now that's a kind
of shopping any guy can get behind!

For example:
- CHOOSING A STEAK.
- ESTABLISHING THE PERFECT PIZZA-TOPPING COMBO.
- DETERMINING WHAT TO HAVE ON YOUR BURGER.
- FINDING THE PERFECT LOBSTER IN THE TANK.
- ORDERING A BURRITO.

Diets, cholesterol, sodium, that one kind of blowfish
that will kill you when not prepared properly...
These concerns should not bother you.
Nothing should bother you when you're eating—
as anyone who's gotten too near your plate already knows.

Now you're talking (with your mouth full)!

PLACE WITH COOL STUFF
DIGITAL STORE

This is a magical time to be a guy. Our ancestors had to go outside to find things. No more!

The entire world is yours online. Pretty much anything you can think of can be typed into a browser, and then it will basically shop for itself. Music, movies, your favorite TV show from back in the day… All of this and more is available in digital form.

Why is digital cooler than whatever we called stuff
before digital? That's the kind of question a guy
like you does not ask. Why do you need the remastered
versions of everything you already have?
Again with the not asking.

YOU DESERVE THE MOST MASTERFUL MASTERING AVAILABLE.
IMPOSSIBLY COOL, BRUSHED-ALUMINUM CASE CLOSED.

So now that you've got some ideas on where to go,

How about getting yourself some cool stuff?

It's going to take a big person to wade through all the options and choose the very best, most perfect thing. But you are that person! Believe in yourself, trust your instincts, and remember, no sale is final.